WASHINGTON HUSKIES

BY
RAMEY TEMPLE

INSIDE COLLEGE FOOTBALL

MEDIA ENHANCED BOOKS
AV2 BY WEIGL
ADDED VALUE • AUDIO VISUAL
www.av2books.com

Published by AV² by Weigl
350 5th Avenue, 59th Floor
New York, NY 10118
Website: www.av2books.com

Library of Congress Control Number: 2018968205

ISBN 978-1-7911-0075-9 (hardcover)
ISBN 978-1-7911-0076-6 (multi-user eBook)
ISBN 978-1-7911-0077-3 (single-user eBook)

Printed in Guangzhou, China
1 2 3 4 5 6 7 8 9 0 23 22 21 20 19

042019
102318

Project Coordinator: Jared Siemens Designer: Terry Paulhus

Every reasonable effort has been made to trace ownership and to obtain permission to reprint copyright material. The publishers would be pleased to have any errors or omissions brought to their attention so that they may be corrected in subsequent printings.

The publisher acknowledges Alamy, Getty Images, Newscom, and Wikimedia Commons as its primary image suppliers for this title.

INSIDE COLLEGE FOOTBALL

Washington Huskies

CONTENTS

Introduction

The University of Washington (UW) Huskies are a Pacific-12 (Pac-12) Conference football team with loyal fans and one of the loudest stadiums in college football. They compete in one of the toughest conferences in college football. When the Huskies play the Washington State University Cougars, the entire state of Washington seems to be watching. This game is known as the Apple Cup. The teams have been meeting at the Apple Cup for more than 100 years. Although the Huskies have won most of the **matchups**, the games are always hard-fought and close in score.

The Huskies have been led by some very successful coaches. Jim Owens and Don James are two of the best-known. They both helped the Huskies to several Rose Bowls, and James helped the Huskies get to their only **National Championship** win. Under the current leadership of Chris Petersen, the Huskies are a much-talked-about team and look ready to win some championships.

Washington quarterback Jake Browning recorded a career 11,983 passing yards and 94 touchdowns during his four seasons in a Huskies uniform.

Salvon Ahmed was one of seven UW players who saw playing time as a true freshman. He recorded 388 rushing yards and three touchdowns as the Huskies' backup running back in 2017.

W

WASHINGTON

Stadium Alaska Airlines Field at Husky Stadium

Division Pacific-12 (Pac-12) North

Head Coach Chris Petersen

Location Seattle, Washington

National Championships 1

Nicknames Dawgs, U-Dub

3
Pro Football Hall of Famers

18
Conference Championships

38
Bowl Appearances

73
Apple Cup Championships

History

The Huskies have won 7 of the 15 Rose Bowls they have played.

The 1990 Huskies earned a sixth Rose Bowl victory when they defeated the Iowa Hawkeyes 46–34.

The Huskies played their first football game in 1889. The **iconic** Husky Stadium was built in 1920 to accommodate the growing football program. In 1923, the Huskies beat the Navy Midshipmen to capture their first-ever Rose Bowl win. The team rose to prominence when Coach Jim Owens took over the program in the late 1950s. Owens coached the team for nearly 20 seasons. Under his leadership, they won back-to-back Rose Bowls in 1959 and 1960.

The Dawgs rose to greater heights under Coach Don James, who took over in 1975 and built the Huskies into a powerhouse. He led them to many bowl wins. They won the 1977 and 1981 Rose Bowls. Many people claim 1991 was the best year for the Dawgs, as they finished the season undefeated. They won the Rose Bowl and were declared National Champions.

In 1994, Jim Lambright led the Huskies to the Orange Bowl. The crushing win against the University of Miami became known as the "Whammy in Miami." The early 2000s brought another Rose Bowl victory for the Huskies. Current head coach Chris Petersen took over in 2014, and the Huskies quickly won the Pac-12 Championship. Hopes are high for the Dawgs as Petersen settles into his coaching role.

A statue of legendary Huskies coach Jim Owens was placed in front of Husky Stadium in 2003. Owens boasts the second-most wins in UW history.

The Stadium

Husky Stadium was home to the Seattle Seahawks while the Seahawks' stadium was being constructed. The Seahawks' owner, the late Paul Allen, financed several upgrades to Husky Stadium during this time.

Husky Stadium opened in 1920, replacing Denny Field as the Dawgs' home. It was built with a U-shaped design. This design allows fans to see views of Lake Washington and Mount Rainier. The stadium is one of a handful of college stadiums that are accessible by water. Fans are able to come to the game by boat.

Husky Stadium has hosted several National Football League (NFL) games. The Seattle Seahawks played all of their home games there during the 2000 and 2001 seasons. The stadium has also been recognized as one of the loudest college football stadiums. During a 1992 game against the University of Nebraska, the noise level reached 133.6 **decibels**. That's almost as loud as a jet plane taking off.

A $280 million **remodel** was completed in 2013. It included new seating, new concession stands, and new bathrooms. In 2015, Alaska Airlines bought the naming rights to the stadium. Husky Stadium is now officially called the Alaska Airlines Field at Husky Stadium. However, students and fans continue to call it Husky Stadium.

Washington fans can avoid the crowded stadium parking and take a boat to the game. Fans can anchor their own boats in the bay next to the stadium and take a shuttle boat to the game.

Where They Play

Welcome to Husky Stadium, where more than 70,000 people gather to watch the Washington Huskies play on Alaska Airlines Field. Fans come by car and boat and fill the stands with purple and gold. They raise their voices to cheer for their team and stomp their feet in celebration, helping to make Husky Stadium the loudest in college football.

PAC-12 NORTH

1. **Oregon State University**
   Corvallis, Oregon
2. **Stanford University**
   Stanford, California
3. **University of California**
   Berkeley, California
4. **University of Oregon**
   Eugene, Oregon
5. ★ **University of Washington**
   Seattle, Washington
6. **Washington State University**
   Pullman, Washington

Arena
Alaska Airlines Field at Husky Stadium

Location
Seattle, Washington

Broke Ground
May 17, 1920

Completed
November 27, 1920

Surface
Artificial Turf

Features
- The stadium's seating capacity is 70,138
- One of the first-ever audience "waves" took place at the stadium on Halloween night, 1981
- There is a bronze statue of Coach Don James in the northwest plaza outside Husky Stadium

PAC-12 SOUTH

1. **Arizona State University**
   Tempe, Arizona
2. **University of Arizona**
   Tucson, Arizona
3. **University of California, Los Angeles**
   Los Angeles, California
4. **University of Colorado Boulder**
   Boulder, Colorado
5. **University of Southern California**
   Los Angeles, California
6. **University of Utah**
   Salt Lake City, Utah

WASHINGTON
OREGON
IDAHO
MONTANA
NORTH DAKOTA
SOUTH DAKOTA
WISCONSIN
MINNESOTA
WYOMING
IOWA
NEBRASKA
NEVADA
UTAH
COLORADO
KANSAS
MISSOURI
CALIFORNIA
OKLAHOMA
ARKANSAS
ARIZONA
NEW MEXICO
TEXAS
LOUISIANA
Pacific Ocean
N
S
E
W
SCALE
0 miles
500 miles
0 kilometers
500 km
LEGEND
Home Stadium
Pac-12 North
Pac-12 South
United States
Other Countries
Water

The Uniforms

One of the **helmets** that Nike made for the Huskies had a texture representing the **frost** of the Pacific Northwest.

The triangular points under the shoulders of Husky jerseys represent the unique "jaws" formed by the roofline of Husky Stadium.

The Huskies uniform has changed many times over the years. However, the uniforms have remained fairly similar since 1975 and the arrival of Coach Don James. The traditional home uniform is a purple jersey with white numbers and gold pants. The helmets are gold with a purple W.

The Huskies wear other uniforms as well, depending on the game being played. For example, the Huskies may wear black or white pants. They also have jerseys and helmets in many different colors. They have even been known to wear chrome helmets. All of these uniform options are called "alternate uniforms." Alternate uniforms can be worn at different times throughout the season.

In 2018, the Huskies ended their uniform contract with Nike. Nike had been making the Husky uniforms for 20 years. In 2019, Adidas is introducing brand-new uniforms.

Former Huskies head coach Jim Owens introduced purple helmets in the 1960s. They have appeared in games at various times in the team's history ever since.

Student Athletes

Only about **2 percent** of college students in the United States are awarded athletic scholarships.

In wide receiver Dante Pettis's final year as a Husky, he tallied 1,256 receiving yards. He also scored 24 touchdowns over his four seasons at UW.

Being a college student athlete is hard work. Student athletes have to perform well on the football field and in the classroom. Colleges have many services to help student athletes succeed. Student athletes are provided with academic counseling, mentoring, and tutors.

Many student athletes are given athletic scholarships. An athletic scholarship is a financial aid agreement between the athlete and the college or university. Athletes who do not receive an athletic scholarship can be "walk-on" members of the team. This means they are on the team, but without athletic financial aid. The UW athletic department typically awards the maximum number of football scholarships allowed, which is 85.

Brayden Dickey had 452 receiving yards, 42 receptions, and three touchdowns over 40 games during his time at Washington.

Bowl Games

Washington has ended **every season** since 2010 with a bowl game.

The Huskies won the 2015 Heart of Dallas Bowl with a 44–31 win over the University of Southern Mississippi.

Bowl games are **postseason** games that count toward the national title claim. There are 40 college football bowl games and the National Championship game. The bowl games happen after the conference championships. Since 2014, the College Football Playoff Selection Committee matches up four teams. The top four teams compete in two semifinal bowl games. The winners of those games advance to the National Championship.

The Huskies have played in many different bowls over the years, including the Rose Bowl, the Holiday Bowl, and the Sun Bowl. They have played in almost 40 bowl games. Of all the bowls, they have played in the Rose Bowl the most often. Coach James led them to the most bowl games, including three back-to-back Rose Bowls. Most recently, they played in the 2019 Rose Bowl. Their bowl record is 17–20–1.

Washington and Pennsylvania State University had identical records going into the 2017 Fiesta Bowl, but the Huskies lost 28–35.

The Coaches

In 2017, Coach Chris Petersen signed a **contract extension** with the Huskies. He is guaranteed to be head coach through the 2023 season.

In 2016, Chris Petersen led Washington to one of the best seasons in program history, which included the Huskies' first-ever College Football Playoff game and their first 12-win finish since 1991.

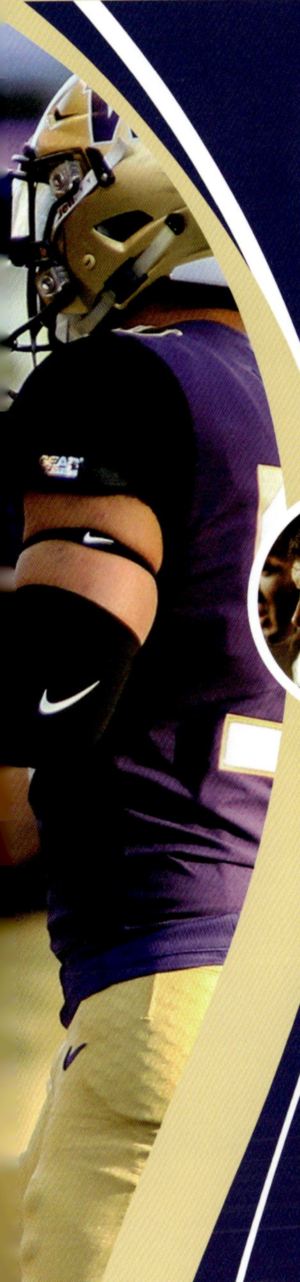

Huskies football has largely been defined by a handful of head coaches. During the 1950s and throughout his many seasons with the Dawgs, Jim Owens maintained a winning record. Don James took over after Owens, continuing to build on his successful program. The current head coach, Chris Petersen, was hired with the goal of winning another National Championship. Dawgs fans are hoping Petersen will be remembered as another Husky coaching legend.

JIM OWENS Jim Owens was the head Husky coach from 1957 to 1974. Under his leadership, the Huskies won three Athletic Association of Western Universities titles and went to the Rose Bowl three times. He helped UW win its very first Rose Bowl in 1960 against Wisconsin. Owens was inducted into the Husky Hall of Fame in 1979.

DON JAMES Don James took over in 1975 and remained head coach for 18 seasons. He led the team to 15 different bowl games, including four Rose Bowl wins. During his time, the Dawgs also won 99 Pacific-10 Conference (Pac-10) victories and a National Championship. James retired after Washington's 1992 season and was inducted into the College Football Hall of Fame in 1997.

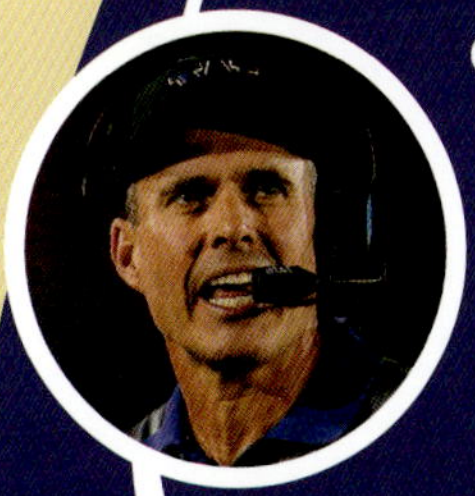

CHRIS PETERSEN Chris Petersen is the current head coach of the Washington Huskies. He began coaching in 2014. The Huskies have won a Pac-12 Championship under Petersen and appeared in a College Football Playoff. Petersen was the winner of the Stallings Award. This award is given to excellent coaches who are also great humanitarians.

The Mascot

Dubs II's training to become the Huskies mascot included learning to run out of the tunnel before games, getting used to the roar of the crowd at Husky Stadium, and tolerating the fireworks that are sometimes used at games.

The Huskies have two mascots. One is a live dog. The first live dog mascot, Frosty, debuted in 1922. Frosty was an Alaskan Husky who lived on campus with a fraternity and attended all of Washington's football games. The current mascot is Dubs II, and he is UW's 14th live mascot. Dubs II, an Alaskan Malamute, took over for the previous mascot, Dubs, after the 2018 season ended. Dubs II was adopted by a local UW family, who taught him all he needs to know to be the next Huskies mascot.

The second Huskies mascot is Harry the Husky. This body suit-costumed mascot made his debut in 1995. Harry the Husky wears a purple and gold football uniform and wows the crowd with his animated dance moves.

The students who play Harry the Husky have a demanding schedule. Harry appears at football, basketball, and volleyball home games, as well as various school and community events. Harry also attends many football away games.

Legends of the Past

For many players, their time with the Huskies is the start of a promising football career. These are some of the best-known football players to play for the University of Washington.

Napoleon Kaufman

Napoleon Kaufman played for the Huskies in the early 1990s. Kaufman was UW's all-time rush leader. He was also a three-time All-Pac-10 pick, and in his senior year, he was a second-team **All-American**. In 2004, Kaufman was inducted into the Husky Hall of Fame. He was **drafted** in the first round by the Los Angeles Raiders in 1995, just before the team moved back to Oakland. He went on to play in the NFL for six years. Kaufman ranks 11th in the NFL all-time rushing average, with 4.9 yards per carry.

Position: Running Back
Seasons: 1991–1994 (UW Huskies), 1995–2000 (Oakland Raiders)
Born: June 7, 1973, Kansas City, Missouri

Steve Emtman

Steve Emtman was a Husky on the 1991 undefeated National Championship team. During his years at UW, he won both the Outland Trophy and the Lombardi Award, which are both awarded to the best college football lineman in the country. Emtman was the number-one overall NFL Draft pick in 1992. He played in the NFL for the Indianapolis Colts, Miami Dolphins, and Washington Redskins. He retired after the 1997 season. Emtman was inducted into the College Football Hall of Fame in 2006.

Position: Defensive Tackle and Defensive End
Seasons: 1988–1991 (UW Huskies), 1992–1994 (Indianapolis Colts), 1995–1996 (Miami Dolphins), 1997 (Washington Redskins)
Born: April 16, 1970, Spokane, Washington

Bishop Sankey

Bishop Sankey played running back for UW for three seasons. In 2012, he was named the **Most Valuable Player (MVP)** at the Maaco Bowl and was an honorable mention All-Pac-12. After his junior season, he entered the NFL Draft. Sankey was a second-round draft pick for the Tennessee Titans. He played for the Titans for two seasons. He was then signed to the practice squads of the New England Patriots, Kansas City Chiefs, and Minnesota Vikings. In 2018, Sankey signed with the San Diego Fleet of the Alliance of American Football League.

Position: Running Back
Seasons: 2011–2013 (UW Huskies), 2014–2015 (Tennessee Titans), 2019 (San Diego Fleet)
Born: September 15, 1992, Wadsworth, Ohio

Budda Baker

Budda Baker played three seasons as a Husky. He was a strong safety who led the Huskies with 71 tackles in his junior year. In 2016, he was an NCAA Consensus All-American and a first-team All-American. After his junior year, Baker decided to enter the NFL Draft. He was picked 36th overall by the Arizona Cardinals. In his first NFL season, Baker was one of four Cardinals named to the 2018 **Pro Bowl**. Baker signed a four-year deal with the Cardinals. He will be playing with them through the 2020 season.

Position: Safety
Seasons: 2014–2016 (UW Huskies), 2017–Present (Arizona Cardinals)
Born: January 10, 1996, Bellevue, Washington

All-Time Records

5,323
Career Rushing Yards
In 2018, Myles Gaskin sealed his name in UW's record books with his 5,323 career rushing yards. He beat Napoleon Kaufman's prior record of 4,106 yards.

243
Career Receptions
Receiver Reggie Williams set the UW record for career receptions, with 243. He also holds UW's records for career receiving yards and receiving yards per game.

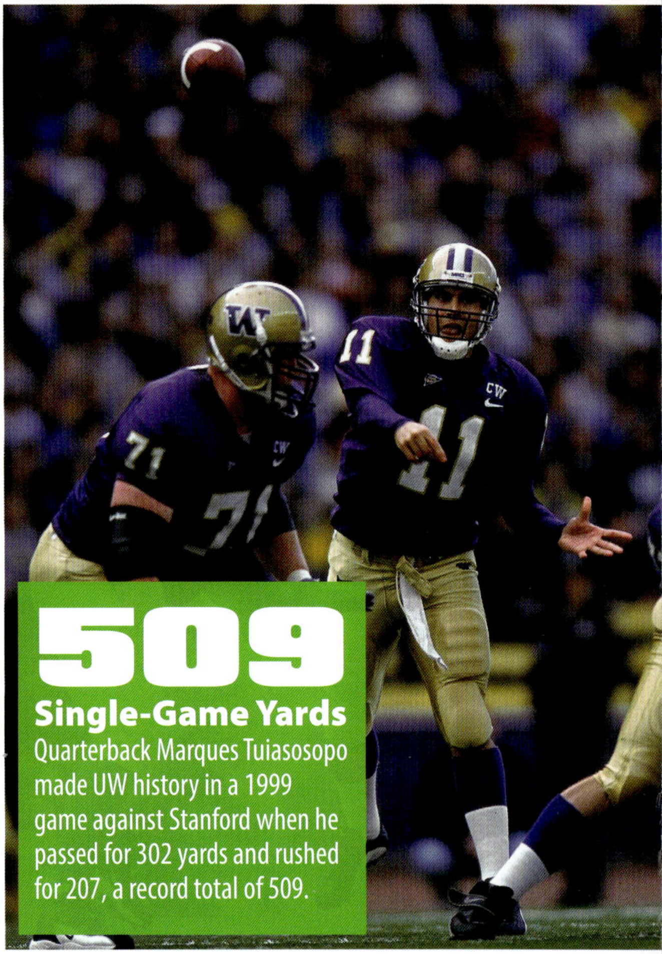

509
Single-Game Yards
Quarterback Marques Tuiasosopo made UW history in a 1999 game against Stanford when he passed for 302 yards and rushed for 207, a record total of 509.

57

Career Rushing Touchdowns

With 57 rushing touchdowns, Myles Gaskin holds the Huskies record for most career rushing touchdowns.

10,347

Career Passing Yards

Quarterback Jake Browning broke the 15-year school record for career passing yards, with 10,347 yards in September 2018.

Timeline

Throughout the team's history, the Washington Huskies have had many memorable events that have become defining moments for the team and its fans.

1889
The Huskies play their first football game on Thanksgiving Day.

1920
Husky Stadium is built.

1900 | 1920 | 1940 | 1960

UW plays Washington Agricultural College, now Washington State University, in what is the first Apple Cup game.

1960
UW wins the Rose Bowl by defeating the Wisconsin Badgers, who were the reigning National Champions.

1975
Legendary coach Don James is hired.

1991
The Huskies have an undefeated season and are declared National Champions.

1992
A game played at Husky Stadium against the University of Nebraska reaches 133.6 decibels, the loudest college football game on record.

1980 2000 2020

2001
The Huskies win their eighth Rose Bowl.

In 2014, head coach Chris Petersen is hired.

2016
The Dawgs win the Pac-12 Championship.

The Future
Heading into the future, there are great expectations for the Washington Huskies. The team has earned a reputation for winning in recent seasons, and returning veteran players will keep the Huskies on top. Coach Petersen is a well-liked coach who is priming the Dawgs for another championship run.

Write a Biography

Life Story

A person's life story can be the subject of a book. This kind of book is called a biography. Biographies often describe the lives of people who have achieved great success. These people may be alive today, or they may have lived many years ago. Reading a biography can help you learn more about a great person.

Get the Facts

Use this book, and research in the library and on the internet, to find out more about your favorite player. Learn as much about him as you can. What position does he play? What are his statistics in important categories? Has he set any records? Also, be sure to write down key events in the person's life. What was his childhood like? What has he accomplished off the field? Is there anything else that makes this person special or unusual?

Use the Concept Web

A concept web is a useful research tool. Read the questions in the concept web on the following page. Answer the questions in your notebook. Your answers will help you write a biography.

Concept Web

Write a Biography

Adulthood
- Where does this individual currently reside?
- Does he have a family?

Your Opinion
- What did you learn from the books you read in your research?
- Would you suggest these books to others?
- Was anything missing from these books?

Childhood
- Where and when was this person born?
- Describe his parents, siblings, and friends.
- Did he grow up in unusual circumstances?

Accomplishments off the Field
- What is this person's life's work?
- Has he received awards or recognition for accomplishments?
- How have this person's accomplishments served others?

Help and Obstacles
- Did this individual have a positive attitude?
- Did he receive help from others?
- Did this person have a mentor?
- Did this person face any hardships?
- If so, how were the hardships overcome?

Accomplishments on the Field
- What records does this person hold?
- What key games and plays have defined his career?
- What are his stats in categories important to his position?

Work and Preparation
- What was this person's education?
- What was his work experience?
- How does this person work?
- What is the process he uses?

Trivia Time

Take this quiz to test your knowledge of the Washington Huskies. The answers are printed upside down under each question.

1 Which NCAA division do the Huskies compete in?

A. The Pac-12 North

2 What is the name of the stadium where the Huskies play?

A. Alaska Airlines Field at Husky Stadium

3 What is the name of the annual game played between UW and the Washington State Cougars?

A. The Apple Cup

4 When did the Huskies win their only National Championship?

A. 1991

5 Which coach is memorialized with a bronze statue at Husky Stadium?

A. Coach Don James

6 How many people can Husky Stadium hold?

A. 70,138

7 Who are the Outland Trophy and Lombardi Award given to?

A. The best college lineman in the country

8 What are the names of the two Husky mascots?

A. Dubs/Dubs II and Harry the Husky

9 Which bowl game have the Huskies played in the most?

A. The Rose Bowl

10 What type of dog is Dubs II?

A. An Alaskan Malamute

Key Words

All-American: a player, usually in high school or college, judged to be the best in each position of a sport

decibels: the unit used to measure sound

drafted: chosen to play professionally in the National Football League during an annual event

iconic: famous or well-known

matchups: contests between two athletes or sports teams

Most Valuable Player (MVP): the player judged to be most valuable to his team's success

National Championship: the top achievement for any sport or contest in a particular nation

postseason: a sporting event that takes place after the end of the regular season

Pro Bowl: the annual all-star game for NFL players pitting the best players in the National Football Conference against the best players in the American Football Conference

remodel: to improve or expand an existing building

Index

Log on to www.av2books.com

AV² by Weigl brings you media enhanced books that support active learning. Go to www.av2books.com, and enter the special code found on page 2 of this book. You will gain access to enriched and enhanced content that supplements and complements this book. Content includes video, audio, weblinks, quizzes, a slideshow, and activities.

AV² Online Navigation

Audio
Listen to sections of the book read aloud.

Book Pages
AV² pages directly correspond to pages in the book.

Video
Watch informative video clips.

Embedded Weblinks
Gain additional information for research.

Key Words
Study vocabulary, and complete a matching word activity.

Try This!
Complete activities and hands-on experiments.

Quizzes
Test your knowledge.

Slideshow
View images and captions, and prepare a presentation.

AV² was built to bridge the gap between print and digital. We encourage you to tell us what you like and what you want to see in the future.

Sign up to be an AV² Ambassador at www.av2books.com/ambassador.

Due to the dynamic nature of the internet, some of the URLs and activities provided as part of AV² by Weigl may have changed or ceased to exist. AV² by Weigl accepts no responsibility for any such changes. All media enhanced books are regularly monitored to update addresses and sites in a timely manner. Contact AV² by Weigl at 1-866-649-3445 or av2books@weigl.com with any questions, comments, or feedback.